UGLY DUCKLING PRESSE :: DOSSIER

Ventrakl
© Christian Hawkey 2010, 2013, 2017

ISBN: 978-1-933254-64-7

Library of Congress Cataloging-in-Publication Data

Hawkey, Christian, 1969-
  Ventrakl / Christian Hawkey. -- 1st ed.
     p. cm.
  Poems.
  ISBN 978-1-933254-64-7 (pbk. : alk. paper)
  I. Title.
  PS3608.A89V46 2010
  811'.6--dc22

                          2010031702

Distributed to the trade by
Small Press Distribution / SPD
1341 Seventh Street, Berkeley, CA 94710
www.spdbooks.org

Available directly from UDP and through our partner bookstores.

This book is funded in part by an award from the National Endowment for the Arts, and by public
funds from the New York City Department of Cultural Affairs in partnership with the City Council.

First Edition 2010
Second Printing 2013
Third Printing 2017
Printed in the USA

Ugly Duckling Presse
The Old American Can Factory
232 Third Street #E303
Brooklyn, NY 11215

www.uglyducklingpresse.org

NATIONAL
ENDOWMENT
FOR THE ARTS

VENTRAKL

Christian Hawkey | Georg Trakl

[a collaboration]

PREFACE

Au contraire d'une fonction de numéraire facile et représentatif, comme le traite d'abord la foule, le dire, avant tout rêve et chant, retrouve chez le Poëte, par nécessité constitutive d'un art consacré aux fictions, sa virtualité.

—Mallarmé

Ask ye what ghost I dream upon?

—Pound, "Villonaud for This Yule"

Voices pass through consciousness, sometimes called upon, other times without request. Often they are the recorded and randomly stored voices of the living—a friend, a neighbor, someone who, the day before, heckled you from a passing car window. For me, the voice of Arnold Schwarzenegger saying "I'll be back" is a frequent, not altogether unwelcome auditory hallucination. Our bodies, our heads, our skulls, the holes in our bodies and skulls are voice chambers, sound chambers, wherein our own voiced selves and the voiced selves of others constantly enter and exit, and are changed by our bodies upon entrance, exit. Consciousness, at least metonymically, is voiced, and the voice, as Mladen Dolar has suggested, is less a vehicle for "self-presence" than a void, a blank space at the site of intersection.

What happens when those voices are of the deceased? When a parent, for example, long since passed away, suddenly calls your name? What happens, further, in the case of poems written nearly a full century ago? To read is to animate words, let them speak with you, alongside you, as you. To read a poem is to allow a text and its voiced accents (timbres, tonations) to unfold within one's reading voice, thereby forming a loop, a voice-over—a between voice. Bachelard: "One feature of the spoken image is sufficient for us to read the poem as an echo of a vanished past." And to read the deceased is to reanimate their words; the between-voice is a ghost, a host.

Books—of the living or the dead—are the truest ghosts among us, the immaterial made material. And this book is a ghost containing a ghost: a collaboration with the German poet Georg Trakl, who died in 1914. Trakl knew, as Heidegger knew, that the *ghostly* is not a spiritual state, but a being between states, a "being terrified, a being beside himself, *ek-static*." In this sense, collaboration between the living and the dead is the meeting of ghosts because writing is, in the purest sense, an act that sets the fiction of one's self aside. It is also a form of friendship. Agamben: "Friendship is this desubjectivication at the very heart of the most intimate sensation of the self." And in taking up multiple procedures of writing and translation—transwriting, transrelating—one aim was to prolong the friendship of our ghosts as long as possible.

When I was working on this book, I did not yet speak or read German. This made it somewhat hard to talk! And this was precisely why I wanted to talk: to cross a boundary, a border. Translation in the general sense occurs in any encounter with a text, an image, a face, a sound, an idea, a traffic light. Concerning the translation of poems—a form of ghostly reanimation—the critical writing that constitutes an argument against literal or overly faithful translations is now nearly as large as its extant supporting examples. Celan, translating Dickinson, radically altered some lines. Such willful mistranslation is of course a precise act of fidelity to the space which Dickinson's poems point to (Spicer: "I would like to point to the real, disclose it, to make a poem that has no sound in it but the pointing of a finger"). It's also something at the heart of any inspired writing: by clearing such a space, a linguistic utterance offers an invitation to enter, to collaborate, to fill or fill out the pointed-to space. Indexicality is, in this sense, spatial hope—a space defined by possibility ("an arrangement in a system to pointing," writes Stein). In the case of Trakl's work I was interested in approaching it and pointing to it (including the use of sound as the only finger) from as many locations as possible, in part to trouble Benjamin's distinctions between poet and translator, between a language forest's center (where works of literature lie) and translations (which lie outside that center and call "into it without entering it"). If such distinctions were decentered, or blurred, what would *that* reality look like, feel like, spell? What space— circling inside the outskirts of German—could one inhabit? In the case of his life I was also interested in starting from a non-linguistic space: images, and most importantly, photographs. What traces or traces of a life could I find there, translate there? Does one defer to the magic of the photograph, the weirdly doubled aura of the historical author portrait? Can one engage it actively, generatively, using writing and the visual editing and manipulation tools now packaged into all our writing technology (crop, rotate, enlarge) to either exaggerate its magic or dispel it? Both?

For the poems here, the modes of composition deployed are numerous and varied. Some were composed by combing through all of Trakl's available poems in English for lines in which a given color appears; I then rearranged, cut, and altered (slightly) the lines to build poems—centos. No poet before or after Trakl deployed such a limited set of colors so frequently and suggestively and without any apparent fixed cosmology of meaning. Nearly every stanza of every one of his poems contains color as valence, and at some point I realized my procedure was exploring the poetics of inventory as yet another translation mode. Other procedures involved the generation of what might be called homo*graph*onic drafts (building on the growing tradition of homophonic translation), where a word (or words) from one's native language is identified within a foreign word or text by either sound or sight (i.e. one sees and/or hears *ends* or *bends* or *sonnet* cradled within *abendsonate*), in part because the textual surface of an unknown language becomes so intensely visual. Sometimes, inspired by a procedure invented by the poet David Cameron, I typed into Microsoft Word a Trakl poem in German and used the spell check program to produce an initial draft. Other strategies involved typing the poem into an online translation engine and then translating the poem back and forth, line by line, between English and German; or shooting, with a 12 gauge, an open Trakl book from a distance of ten feet, then translating, with a dictionary, a remaining page of perforated text. Still other poems were generated by working from a book of Trakl's poems which I had left outside to decompose over a full year in a glass jar filled with rainwater and leaves and mosquito larvae until its pages, over time, dissolved into words, pieces of words, word-stems, floating up and rearranging themselves on the surface of the jar.

There were many other techniques, starting points and constraints, all of which allowed for the privilege of departing from them. Above all, I let Trakl enter the space of the following texts whenever he felt so inclined. On rare occasions, after composing a poem or series of poems, we conducted a brief meeting—an interview. Always, when I went looking for him, he was there. The room we eventually abandoned is anyone's to inhabit. Ultimately these are not my poems. Nor are they Trakl's. They occur at some site between our languages, texts, names, as well as between our (ghostly) bodies redoubled by the erotics of collaboration and translation.

A more fixed but mutual site is war: my own American English, infiltrated daily by the ongoing wars in Iraq and Afghanistan, and Trakl's German, which traced, in poem after poem, the increasing, collective anxiety generated by a European landscape (and poetic tradition) being absorbed—erased—by the industrial revolution, culminating in his own horrifyingly direct experience with the first machine-based war of the 20th century. Given the current condition of permanent, technology-driven global warfare, it was and sadly is an anxiety I share. It's why I started reading him again in the first place— to find, across a century, a locus of resonant and courageous melancholy.

—Christian Hawkey
South Kortright, NY
June 23, 2006

Possible
To use
Words provided one treat them
As enemies.
Not enemies—Ghosts.

—George Oppen

Grasp: translate. And everything is translation at every level, in every direction.

—Henri Michaux, *Stroke by Stroke*
(translation: Richard Sieburth)

Golden cloud and time. In a lonely room
You often ask the dead to visit you.

—Georg Trakl, "To One Who Died Young"
(translation: Daniel Simko)

In any strange land I would
read you, even at home.

—Robert Walser, "To Georg Trakl"
(translation: Uljana Wolf)

VENTRAKL

÷

NEITHER OF US IS POWERLESS

You are, clearly, on a beach, and judging by the diminutive waves and the soft, brushed surface of the water it is a lake, or a small sea, Lake Como perhaps, or the Black Sea.

How is such a narrative possible—the mother and two children in the background, for example, standing (it seems) on the surface of the mineral-heavy water; the mother lowers a string into the depths, the boy tilts toward her, the girl stands one step back from the hole. Here, then, is a triangle: The mother addicted to drugs, the sister who was the only person who understood you, who became an alcoholic and shot herself and you, leaning forward as if running—or falling—into the hole, the chloroform hole, the cigarette hole, the opium hole, the morphine hole, the veronal hole, the cocaine hole, the mouth hole, the nose hole, the vein hole, the food hole, the language hole, breathing hole, word hole. Here, as if the figures are held behind your back, in the palm of your hand, a history, a history of holes and what we put inside them, lose inside them. You claim that until the age of 20 you noticed nothing in your environment save for water. Perhaps, then, you were falling through it or through the word for it, bottomless—

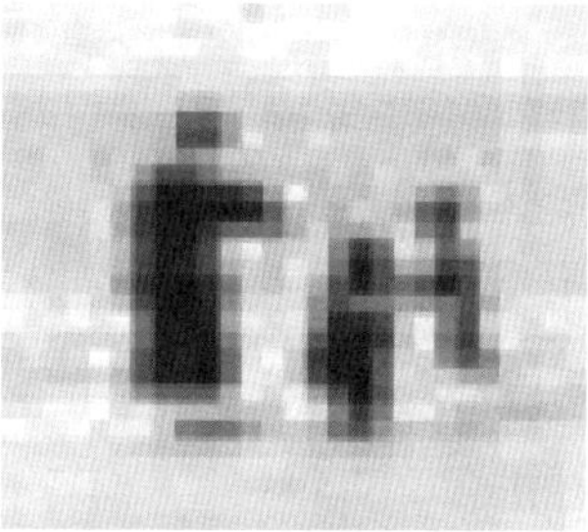

when your own posture, however, offers no discernible narrative. You seem and do not seem to be speaking. You seem and do not seem to be listening to someone outside the frame. You seem and do not seem to be holding a cigarette, the chewed end of a cigar, a shell. It seems to me a small camera pointed at the one taking the photograph, the one for whom you pretend not to be posing.

I see you, you seem to say. Neither of us is powerless.

In summer utterance: orphans
Of stillness-mittens. Without ant-light
In a green world, a glass of wine
Offers vertical stars, offers
A handful of tiny, wilted ears.

I am willing to teach my sister
Zeros lie around wondrous bends.
Our mother is a shuffling singer.
A gaunt water-shaft. A two-way river.
I am humming to a gelatinous king.

Again Fall glitters in locked cellars
Where smooth, river-polished stones
Glow in the wide mouths of toddlers.
These children fluster my inner night.

When we address each other we do not use names, have never used names. We are both equally tired of them, weary of them, the way one wearies of the same taste, the same food, the same brand of food. And the space in which we meet? It can most easily be described as a room, a nearly empty room. It has walls. A drawn curtain. A desk-shaped table with two chairs. The light above the table is real. We sense its heat. There are doors in the room that lead to other rooms, or hallways, which is a word or space between four rooms, at least. Look at it. As always, I am late. Late to this language. I see his back, huge, hunched over the table. Some part of me wants to turn around, to leave, although I feel along the edges of my ears the air pulling me forward. I set my stack of books on the table and slide into the chair across from him. He doesn't move or look up, even though the yellow smoke from his cigarette, held just under his chin, streams directly into his eyes, and disappears into his eyes.

You once, as a child, walked into a pond.

Yes.

And your mother located your body only by the position of your hat
floating on the surface?

The stars at midnight can be a lonely tent.

I see. Submersion, then, becomes a kind of companionship?

The stars at midnight can be a lonely tent.

I'm not sure I follow you....

Listen, can you point me to the nearest whorehouse?

The dead are notoriously hard to satisfy.

—Jack Spicer

÷

AN ARGUMENT FOR ARCHIPELAGOS

TEN HOLES

"the dark one"

"the sick one"

"the patient one"

"the one alone"

"the one sleeping"

"the one dreaming"

"the one watching"

"the one moldering"

"the one observing this"

"the one gone"

Georg Trakl, born in Salzburg, Austria, on February 3, 1887, the fourth of six children, was regarded as the leading poet of German Expressionism. He was rumored to have intimate relations with his own *already you bore me,* although it's more likely that *I saw myself walking through deserted rooms. Dogs howl in the fields. A sister's shadow sways through the silent grove, a dress rustling on the spiral staircase,* what also darkened the days of those years, *you tell me,* moon-bright sonata, the dark gold of rotting sunflowers, ant-light from which at times a gentle animal emerges. A stomach hovers over velvet lawns. *A small blind girl runs trembling down the boulevard.* In the light cast by our sternums *let our song remember the boy.*

I am unfolding a moth into a fluttering mouth, into
The unlimited access of a Visa card.
Dim Wanderer, shining wedge
Of visual decline, your harelip
Smacks of loose jungles, of
Torn, diamond-studded trampolines....

A fleet of tone-deaf geese moves from lock to lock.
Only sounds, dissected, profit you.

DUST ROUNDS

I saw dust mites lurch through deserted rooms.
I saw a tungsten-blue blossom on her sternum.

A plot licks stillness. Dumbness fevers
The last albumen effigies of a miniature world.

Only geese with kindness shimmer
And, once blasted, fall in red blurts.

Down a loneliness-stick inner spangles
Issue tears, and we in unguent failure

Are drawn to this spinsterish ant-light.
Note, for example, the red eyes of sumptuous porters.

The orphans shouting at fences. How they glisten,
At night, with the dimwit mien of an alien order.

WHITETRAKL

A fountain sings. Clouds, white and tender along the edge of night, white birds
Fluttering up the wandering boy's white nightgown.
A white stranger steps into the house. The city's white walls keep ringing.
Softly a white night drifts in
And myrrh blooms silently over the white eyelids of the dead. We meet
With shepherds and white stars. We drink
The white waters of the pool. Mother even carries an infant in her white moon.
Yet more radiant is the white stranger, a white shirt made of stars,
Or, on a cold night, the white cheeks of sisters, their white eyebrows, white heads.

Hole \hohl\ *n* [ME, fr. OE *hol* (fr. Neut. of *hol*, adj., hollow) and *holh*; akin to OHG *hol*, adj., hollow, L *caulis* stalk, stem, Gk *kaulos*] (bef. 12c) **1** a : an opening through something: perforation b : an area where something is missing: gap as (1) : a serious discrepancy : FLAW, WEAKNESS (2) : an opening in a defensive formation; esp. : the area or space between the two front teeth suggesting entrance, permissiveness, or deviancy (3) : a defect in a mouth due to the tongue having left its normal position in one of the crystal bonds and that is equivalent in many respects to a positively charged utterance (4) : a red foliage filled with guitars **2** : a cavity, depression, or hollowed-out place: as a : a cave, pit, or well in the ground b : an unusually deep place in a body of water c : burrow **3** : the suspicion that one's face is being erased in the act of kissing.

He listens in the same position, head down, smoking, unable or unwilling to look up, to look at me. An object passes—slides back and forth—between us. Abend *becomes* "bend," "a bending." Erfüllen *"earfuls" or "sullen elves." Occasionally words like "rough, loose nuns"* (Hoffnungslosen) *make him run his fingers lightly over his shaved head; otherwise, nothing. No flicker of recognition. No sound. We work. Back and forth the words slide, the languages, the words, often the same words: over and over. Who was it who said that a perfect poem could be perfectly translated by a person who didn't know a single word of its language—that the perfect poem has an infinitely small vocabulary? At this point I have no clear idea of what it is we are doing in this room, how we found ourselves here, and I begin to look for reassurances, gestures that might put me at ease, the flicker of a smile, a half-smile, the thoughtful ease with which some people touch their ears, even eye contact—recognition—nothing. As a last resort I begin to watch his lips. They are parted. His tongue may or may not be moving, silently, as he reads. I cannot tell. But the more I look at that space between his lips the more it seems to widen, spread—shadowed and dark, ink-dark, warped.*

The image of a whippoorwill seems significant here.

Yes, exactly, a kind of wild, white foam.

Are mirrors, in that case, factories of sibling rivalry?

I'm not sure. It is unclear whether the story of Cain and Abel prefigured obsidian mirrors.

Perhaps this would explain the love you had for your sister?

I do not comment on undeserted rooms.

Connection then.

I will say this only once: the only sister with whom I've had "intimate relations" is the one inside me, the one who, right now, with these words, speaks.

Is this who I am speaking with?

Don't be so literal. You'll never get anywhere.

Isn't it exactly the opposite?

Then why ask the question.

The question of what?

Of who is speaking.

Who is writing then?

Who is.

Who is.

And the girl who has no song, was given no song by which to remember her save for yours, the ones you wrote, the poems in which the figure of "the sister" appears more than 60 times? *The sister's mouth whispers in black branches.* Sister mouth to brother mouth, brother sun to sister moon. It is a family that remains untranslated—riddled by holes. There is a mouth in this family that cannot speak, that was perhaps always spoken for, an absence where a mouth once was, a sea, or a hole in the sea's fabric: an island. And hence the sadness of an island: subjectivity. Perhaps there is no one "silence" or "void" that words float up from, or over, or across, but rather a particular void for each particular word, particular mouth, and in this case, it is the sister you speak against, that resists any other language but the one her mouth owns, the human noise it owns by remaining firmly closed.

AN ARGUMENT FOR ARCHIPELAGOS

1. As closed ecosystems, islands are laboratories for evolution.

2. And yet: the bigger the island the less it is capable of existing as an island.

3. This fly, for example.

4. Due to inbreeding its eyeballs are enormous—the size of black microphone balls.

5. They are so oversized and heavy it can no longer even fly.

6. When one speaks into a microphone one is really speaking into its diaphragm, a thin piece of material suspended in the ball of the microphone which vibrates when struck by sound.

7. The island would like to make an announcement.

8. It leans into the mic.

9. The mainland, says the island, is a fiction: to see this, all one has to do is fly over it.

10. [The fly, as you can see, records everything in sight.]

The movement of auto-translation, the drive to translate (*Trieb zur Übersetzung*—to use Novalis's term) issues, springs up, not from the *translator* but from this untranslated or this imperfectly translated, which endlessly *demands* translation.

—Jean Laplanche
(translation: Martin Stanton)

÷

BLACK JOY

MELANCHOLIC DECIBELS

—Dear Walt, the verse-orb is breaking.

If a scattered cinder beckons, if a white comet
zithers over our green necks

indecent as a lease
on the glands of Bach, we hum,

veil-light

awkward above our shining sternums.

Umdichtung: not a poem translated from another but a poem woven around another, from another, an image from another image, a weaving or an oscillation around or from, a form of understanding, of knowing that whatever is under you descends, step by step, even if there are no steps, no staircase, nothing to stand on but the soft forehead of a stranger, *O you signs and stars*, your eyes appear to be on the verge of weeping, *if a child can weep*, a face that already sees its future face, sees the soldiers, their cheeks unfolded by shrapnel, sitting up, leaning toward the camera, toward life, a man left in charge of a tent of 90 dying soldiers, *let the song remember the boy,* July 28th, 1914, *March 20th, 2005,* I agree, *wars have their own reunions,* as if violence were its own end, seeking its own form, autonomous, seeking to repeat itself, *a weaving or an oscillation around or from,* form from form, *hence this slow sinking into the forehead of a stranger,* a stranger long departed.

AMEN

Orphans die more gleefully in the green West.
A tapestry made of gelatin. Binary ears.
A hand raised into the wavering trauma-light.

Bright pearls cluster—as if glued—around
The newly opened eyelids of an infant.

Blue lies beneath this all bending, as do
Stunted uncles, kissing. Azrael,

Shaken, backs his red go-cart though the wall.

Later, working intently, my head down, I felt his gaze move over my face—study it. What sense, what hidden sense, alerts us to the fact that we are being observed—not just seen, or glanced at—but watched, steadily. Some say that a caress is the single, most human gesture, and yet he did not move his hands. What I had at first perceived as hostility was, in fact, patience. I knew then that we would be in this room for a long time, that I would return to this room again and again, each time knowing that he would be there, that he had never left.

The landscapes in your poems are always alien, half-empty, emitting a "cold radiance."

Forests, unlike languages, die from the inside out.

And so where do you place yourself?

Where do I place myself? I don't. I am placed—we are placed—in a gorge.

A gorge? A gorgeousness?

Have you ever lain down next to a crib and listened to a burbling infant?

But such speech inscribes nothing.

Exactly.

I'm not sure I understand. Again, the abandoned, often decaying landscapes in your work seem to articulate a sense of impending dread that both responds to the Industrial Revolution and foreshadows the—

I just keep an eye on the animals. The nostrils of a deer at the edge of a forest, for example. They read everything ahead of time, or more immediately in time.

What do you mean by "read."

I mean widen your nostrils when approaching any text.

YELLOWTRAKL

Yellowed with incense the lovers' slight limbs loosen
Shadows on yellow wallpaper; in dark mirrors

The silence of grey clouds, of yellow rocky hills
The sky hardens to grey over the yellow fields

*

Passing along the yellow halls of summer
Yellowing moons roll in silence

Bales of yellow wheat reverberate

Yet she let fall the yellowed curtain
And quietly the yellow corn rustled in the field

A yellow head was bowed, the child lay in stillness

Flies buzz in the yellow vapors
Reeds tremble, yellow and erect

I lean into the paused lips of a stammer-prone orphan;
Ears are tufted; red planets rotate.
Lug nuts and wart hogs on the night-watch. Inner weirdness,
She whispered, fills anyone's jeans with diesel.

Karen, for example, sinks her plump chalcedony into verses
Blue from over-licking. One hand flutters drunkenly in the garden;
Another, bleached by dice-light.

Commodious are the ears of Äpfel.
Gruff the mutterings under Karen's golden buttocks.

O why these kingdoms of mild writing without alternate parks
Where schools of trout move between trees? Why, despite the ant's
        hyacinth-blue light,
This earnest stammering? Blueness
Swells your fuselage, and the Queen's voles,
Dumbstruck by stillness, rotate the stem cells, while Democrats
Moan in the blue light of a lost miner's eyes.

In lieu of guitars, inner trembling. Wild dorks hide in the bushes
Of Holland, in a language tagged with New Balance.
Green trout shift shades; Gibraltar, at night, black as an ant's cheek.

Everyone here aware of where: the photographer is, the lens is, the point toward which the faces lean, converge, swarm the frame, *they do not swarm,* inhabit the frame, *no,* appear as a frame, *better,* or a face, any one face, *its eagerness,* I see you I want to say I *see eyebrows, the muscles beneath them, arranged in a shape we name surprise,* or worry, *that's it,* therefore facial expressions were the first system of, *why first,* surely before human speech evolved—*can you read the space between the flesh that covers the teeth,* you mean the lips, *no the space between them, which a mouth inhabits, delimits, circles, a non-space,* a void perhaps, *don't be pretentious,* what then, *picture someone speaking, now erase the face, the lips in motion, and leave the space between them, widening, shifting, momentarily disappearing,* a shadow, *a moving shadow,* a moving shadow on any surface, *all sensation is a moving surface,* a bird's shadow wrinkling the ocean, *if you like,* in this way we learn to read each other's faces from day one, the moment a shape, oval, hair falling around the light, the waves of light, lowers itself into our field of vision, *odd, territorial phrase,* the space of our own face, *a between space,* what about the tongue, *what about it, all tongues are disgusting.*

German military hospital, WWI, origin unknown.

Someone left you at the crossroads, and for a long time you continue looking back.

—Trakl, "Transformation of Evil"
(translation: Daniel Simko)

One sentence, from one of the few prose poems—among the first in the genre—Trakl wrote. Why "looking back"? Is the "you" looking back along the road he or she came from, accompanied by the "someone" who abandoned the "you"? Is the you looking back at the one who abandons, the trail of departure? And why does the you continue to look back "for a long time"? Heartbreak. Abandonment. Yearning. Shades of Orpheus and Eurydice. And yet to look back for a long time, to look back *continuously* indicates trauma, the inability to move on, move forward, make a choice, step—the non-abled body and its own memory, unwilling or unable to move—step toward healing, forgetfulness. And yet the words are there, were placed there. At the crossroads of the body and language: a placing, a movement that ends in a gesture, a living gesture, even the darkest poems texture us with their own black joy.

1. The surface of the face is the ground of expression.

2. As is, for example, the phrase "an expressionless face."

3. When we write or read or try to translate between languages or make love our faces often look strained, our brows furrowed in concentration, and in some cases our mouths are open and alert—more rounded.

4. We are expressing the fact of a certain position. This position might be stated as follows: communication requires effort.

5. Even writing that sentence I noticed my eyes narrowed, and my lips pursed slightly—no, the corners were drawn outward and slightly up.

6. Eye-narrowing: to ascertain the truth of given statement, a statement coming from someone else's possibly insincere face and that may or may not arrive in the form of words.

7. But we must rephrase this as a question concerning words.

8. And we must be brave in the face of such questions, which in themselves always include the question of words.

9. Do fish suffer from asthma?

REDTRAKL

Red laughter in the dark shade of the chestnuts.
Snow gently drifts from a red cloud.

Crossing in red storms at evening
The mysterious red stillness of your mouth.

Red wolf, strangled by an angel.
Golden red robes, torches, the singing of psalms, the soft rustling
Of red plane trees, red ship on the canal.

We wander quietly along red walls.
Red clouds, spilled blood, gather silently below willow trees.
A red flame leaps from your hand.

÷

TWO WHAT

—and if at this point I look back what in these roads leading away and into you do I know? I know (now) that the photograph of you on the beach was taken in 1913. I know it is the Lido, in Venice. I know you traveled there with two friends: Karl Kraus and Ludwig von Ficker. I know von Ficker was your most loyal supporter, who gave your poems a home in his magazine, who secured for you, during a financial crises, a grant from Ludwig Wittgenstein. I know Wittgenstein professed to understand nothing of your poems. I know he also observed that their tone delighted him, that it was "the tone of true genius." I know you died in a military hospital in Krakow. I know the day you died, the month you died, the year. I know that a few days before this date Wittgenstein, whom you'd never met, was making his way toward you, hoping to meet you, to lift your spirits, give you strength. I know that you once, as a child, walked into a pond. I know that you once, as a child, threw yourself in front of a horse. I know that you once, as a child, threw yourself in front of a train. I know too these are stories, handed down by others, half-truths, myths, and I know you courted and encouraged these myths. I know that you once announced you were going to commit suicide to a friend and the friend, weary of your posing, said "Please, not while I'm around." That you once said *I am only half-born, after all.* That I am—here, now—just as complicit in the construction of your self as your friends were, you were. That I am repeating, reinscribing the myths. I know you were a cocaine addict, a drug addict. I know you worked—no surprise!—at a pharmacy. I know that once, while waiting on customers, you nervously perspired through six changes of shirts. That when von Ficker visited you in the Krakow military asylum he was horrified at the conditions of the inmates, and asked you whether you had any drugs. I know that Wittgenstein also enlisted in the Austrian army, that he was in charge of manning a searchlight on a ship called the *Goplana*, which had been captured from the Russians and was moving along the Vistula river, up into Poland. That he was lonely. That he worked on his theories by the light of this searchlight. I know you loved your younger sister Greta intensely, that she was the only person whose eccentricity was equal to your own—was surpassed by your own, which is why you understood her, admired her, idolized her, protected her, were shattered when you couldn't care for her after a difficult abortion and during her failing health, her failing marriage. I know you inhaled chloroform, drank absinthe, smoked cigarettes dipped in opium, read Rimbaud and Baudelaire and Poe and Verlaine, grew your hair long, wore dandified clothing, courted the "continuous derangement of your senses," pretended to be a *poète maudit*. I know you are one of the first to fall for this pre-packaged, consumable pose, exported by the French Symbolists. I know that, unlike Rimbaud and Mallarmé and Baudelaire, you were one of the first to die of this pre-packaged, consumable myth. "What could he have been," asked Rilke, at first unaware of what you already were, already had achieved. I know you were unbearably lonely in the military hospital, that you heard through von Ficker that Wittgenstein was nearby, and that you immediately wrote to him: *I would be greatly obliged if you would do me the honor of paying a visit . . . I would greatly like to speak with you.* I know you died on the night of November 3rd, 1914, a few days before Wittgenstein arrived. I know that Wittgenstein was in motion, that he was moving toward you. I know I can see this as a line, a moving line, a narrative. I know you were in a cell. A fixed point. I know you were unable to move, move on, construct a narrative stronger than the one the attending doctors constructed for you. I know you were diagnosed with *praecox dementia*, or *schizophrenia*. I know such terms imply an ending, a point from which no one departs. I know that during the battle of Grodek you pressed several times to be sent to the front line. I know you often heard bells ringing. I know that tone takes place in a space adjacent to language. I know that some of your eccentricities were simply the now well-known, clichéd gestures of an addict. I know your sister, Margaret, was also an addict. I know this term means nothing, is empty, says nothing, means only that you were human, that you liked the touch of nicotine, the touch of alcohol, the opium touch, a friend's hand, Wittgenstein's, a stranger's, a strange word—that one feels, reading your poems, touched by words, a touch that moves between languages, a texture, here, I am no one, what is this word, this drive to run through it, let it run through us—windows, how they are willing even at night to work with us. I know you smiled when von Ficker asked if you had drugs in the asylum and replied *how else would I be alive.* That your mother took opium and was more interested in touching the tea cups in her china cabinet than her children. That you failed out of school. That you couldn't hold down a job. That I am repeating, reinscribing the myths. That when you ran out of money you sold your beloved set of Dostoevsky novels in order to afford drugs and alcohol. That you once confessed that you hated your mother enough to murder her with your own hands. I know that the pharmacy was called—fittingly—*The White Angel.* That the overdose of cocaine that killed you was self-administered, a suicide. That in your final letter to von Ficker from the asylum you enclosed your two last poems, "Klage" and "Grodek." I know that of the six children you and your sister Greta looked most alike. I know friends described your tendency to sit without speaking in their presence for hours, then launch into "a monologue as cryptic as his silence." I know that you spent time in brothels. I know that you mostly sat in a corner, drinking, talking to an old prostitute. I know you became precisely what you pretended to be. That here, at least, is one source of your sadness. That the one who dies is not the same as the one who takes his or her own life. That of all the emotions no one ever pretends to be sad. That you were relentlessly earnest. That I am repeating, reinscribing the myths. That there is a space outside of sound. That Wittgenstein, in saying the number two, then asked two what?

High above the earth, in a rotating space lab,
Voles play red guitars
While stem cells gel into
Enzymes, into a somnambulist's face cream.

A duck fart woke the golden Karen. The scattered
Green stomachs of this altitude
Allow unslung weasels to sing gilded vespers,
Allow dustbins of fleas to generate a yellow wind.

Bach is washing a nocturnal Fräulein.
Aussies hang ten on linen waves.
Dear Klein, how completely your mirror-language
Has failed: orphans commit weird acts
While their velvet stomachs hover over the lawns.

In a green locker the severed nerves of voles ring out.
Hungarians touch your private Nissan, whispering
O my dwarf, von Brot, under an herbed wurst.

Today when I enter the room I see his body visibly exhale, release. Usually I feel like an intruder, an outsider, unwelcome, someone to be waved away, as if I'm interrupting something more important, him, his sleep, his dreams, although each time I slip quietly into the seat across from him, watching his eyes and the way they seem to gaze always at some point behind me, beyond me, I think the same thing: this is his dream, not mine. And yet today I feel as if I were late—that he was waiting to begin, or be begun. Stupidly, I wonder if Derrida, as a young boy, ever owned a BB gun, and I think of his late essay where he describes being caught by the gaze of his cat as he stepped naked out of the shower. Undressed in the moment of address. The awareness of fur on my neck. The sense, in a dream, that someone is watching you dream.

You once wrote "the sound of a word expresses an unutterable thought."
Do you see this phonetic experience as the unconscious aspect of language?

I see a red foliage filled with guitars.

Can you be more specific?

No.

Great. I mean, if "the poetic," as Benjamin observes, is something outside
of language, then how is this outside carried over, or re-created, in the
translation of a poem?

Have you ever looked down the throat of a singing orphan?

I haven't, but can you just—

Breathing, the two vocal cords, seen from above, resemble a V. In song they resemble
a red Y.

I'd like to go back to—perhaps it's time to tell you that it was Wittgenstein who, in July of 1914, anonymously sent you money.

If he could have only seen the way my shoulders fell away from my neck.

Yet when you went to the bank to extract the gift you ran away, bathed in sweat, and were never able to return, never returned, in fact, to accept the gift, despite the fact that you were broke?

The shepherd's soft flute needs every one of its holes.

The same gift, I believe, was also made to Rilke, who cashed it out right away.

Well, that was—what is that perfect term in English?—a waste of money.

Schweigen: the silence of one who could speak, but chooses not to, or, since such a choice is another way of speaking—a child's close-lipped, furious gaze—perhaps we should say it is, simply, the silence of one who chooses not to speak for things which have no words, no language, or human language, the language of a cow, for example, when I look into its eye, *into* or *at*, what's the difference, *what's the interior of a cow's eye*, when I look at one of its eyes, at the lubricated, black pupil, surrounded by white, too much white, as if its eyes are permanently swollen, bulging outward, ready for anything that may approach from the side, *the way all animals approach*, its wide, roving gaze *only humans gaze,* its glance then, *that's it,* one-way, *why one,* why not, *just thought I'd ask,* a glance then that expects nothing, requires nothing from what it sees, *surveys,* wordlessly, *the yellow flowers bend without words over the blue pond,* reflections, surfaces, *and yet one sometimes feels that the eyes of the blind are watching them,* I don't understand, *there's a gaze that empties itself of speech, of words, a breathing gaze, where surfaces and faces contract on the inhale, expand on the exhale,* a breathing gaze, *a blue pond,* or a cow's eyeball, *or, alternatively, you could simply bypass the visual by walking up to an eye and simply licking it,* or a text, *yes.*

How beneficial it would be ... to gain a vision of the irreducible differences which a very remote language can, by glimmerings, suggest to us.

—Roland Barthes
(translation: Richard Howard)

REASONS WHY THE BLIND HOVER IN FRONT OF FLOAT GLASS
WINDOWS

1. If the sun is shining: warmth.

2. Even if there is no sun: warmth.

3. *Exempli gratia*: windows, which are made of glass, which is made mostly of quartz, which is otherwise known as sand, which comes most plentifully from the desert.

4. There is a gap in logic in the above statements, but it is not to be found in the way windows perform the same function as a mirage, or the way the faces of the blind lean always toward a heat source.

5. Such as what.

6. Such as someone speaking.

7. Such as someone speaking while they are floating.

8. Such as someone floating out over a surface while they are speaking.

9. Such as some surface floating out over someone while they are speaking.

10. Such as some who speak while out over the one they are speaking to a floating surfaces.

BLUETRAKL

> Clarity sheltered in the dark is blueness.
> —Heidegger
> (translation: Albert
> Hofstadter)

Your face is a blue cloud

Over the gold plains and blue lakes

The blue spring at your feet, the mysterious red stillness of your mouth

Like blue water falling over the rocks

Lean silently over the blue face of a pond

The forehead stirs with the water's blue waves

Blue deer snuffle beneath trees

An angel opens his blue poppy-eyes

A blue moment is even more spirit

And move your arms more beautifully in this blue

And move your arms more beautifully in this blue

Wrapped in his blue coat, a monk from times past

Lives in blue crystal, her cheek leaning on her stars

Blue shapes of people passed through this legend

O how still it all seems walking by the blue river

Silent, god lowers his blue eyelids over

The one moldering, bluishly opening his eyes

And out of a decayed blueness a thing deceased at times emerges

Your legs rattle like blue ice

A blue face quietly leaves you

Drunk on blue scent

Blue flowers

Blue doves

The blue pond

And, as always, blue deer

÷

TRACES

In the evening, the autumn woods resound
with deadly weapons....

—Trakl, "Grodek"
(translation: Daniel Simko)

Two opening lines. Or one opening line, and part of a second line. The first evokes the entire tradition of 19th century European lyric poetry: the season of autumn, of reflection. Woods and forests. Evening. A pastoral landscape of vibrant, resonant melancholy that leads to vibrant, resonant illumination, and the movement from melancholy to illumination is prefigured—announced—by a sound: for example, a shepherd playing a flute, wind in the trees, Aeolus, the god of wind, of inspiration, caressing the strings of the imagination-harp, the language-harp, the poet-as-harp. And yet here, in the second line, the woods ring with something else, something new, something ferociously honest: the mechanized violence of 20th century warfare. The forest (itself a site of endless metaphorical inscriptions—mythic transformation, courtship, the improvised home of bandits and outlaws, or the liberating site, as in Shakespeare, of sex and gender play) now rings with gleaming metal, with steel. There are guns, but the guns are, for the first time, machine guns. 600 rounds a minute. Combat during WWI shifts from choreographed, ephemeral skirmishes to trench warfare. Dig in. Artillery shells. Mortar shells. Death, but with distance, the other at a distance. Bodies no longer fall, are felled, but fall apart, are blown apart—limbs. "Deadly" is an adjective that modifies its own noun.

The poem's title, "Grodek," refers to the battle of Grodek, which took place in Galicia, in what was then Austrian-occupied Poland. The Austrian army, after six days of heavy fighting, was routed by the advancing Russians on September 12th, 1914. It was one of the first battles of WWI and the first in which massive numbers of soldiers were killed. Trakl, assigned to a nearby field hospital as a lieutenant-pharmacist, watched the battle unfold; later he was left in charge—with no physician, no staff, no drugs to ease the pain of those wounded—of 90 wounded and dying soldiers housed in a barn just outside of Grodek. Soldiers, desperate to end their pain, shot themselves. During the Austrian army's chaotic retreat, Trakl also attempted to shoot himself but was caught and disarmed. Within weeks he was transferred to a military hospital in Krakow, where he thought he would work as a pharmacist, although he also feared that he would be court-martialed on grounds of desertion. Instead, he was committed for psychiatric evaluation and determined to be insane.

Two lines. Two worlds. And the words erasing the line between two worlds. The second—mechanized warfare—was not yet a world but only its beginning, and Trakl, who had at the start of the war vehemently requested numerous times to be sent to the front line, ran into it.

The *Maschinengewehr*, a water-cooled machine gun, was a direct copy of the machine gun invented by Hiram Maxim (right), an American inventor. His first patent was for a device called a "hair-curling iron."

Am Abend tönen die herbstlichen Wälder
Von tödlichen Waffen....

I turn to the German. Faced with a foreign language, I do not read it linearly, from left to right, but instead my eye wanders over the words; my ear tracks, skids over sounds, visual parallels to English, probing for lexical similarities, differences—no, just similarities. Herbs. Lichen. Licking. Walden Pond. A bending tone. Toads. Waffles. Curious, random links form and generate their own thought-chains: Walden Pond appears as the site and citation of the back-to-nature, self-sufficient American, and I imagine a *Maschinengewehr* shooting rounds over the surface of the pond, Thoreau stumbling out of his cabin, terrified by the sheer volume of noise, trampling his beloved beans. Even this association lends itself only to ironic contrast; the rest of the words fall back, drift off into randomness, irrelevance, perhaps because this is the poem that, after first encountering it in an essay on Trakl by Heidegger, I am most familiar with. One by one I look the words up in a German-English dictionary. One by one I order the words into a sentence. I begin to sense (reading, translating—attempting to translate) their force, the near-fibrous tension the two lines create between lyricality and mechanized violence, a tension that seems to announce the contours of the coming century. It is also a poem of witness, a poem written by a poet who experienced one of the first battles of WWI. It is a poem that only indirectly bears witness to the poet. This witnessing takes place in the language. In fact, it is this language, the German language. It is also an event, a specific historical event. Maybe this is why the poem resists, resists translation, any form of translation. Or perhaps it demands a specific category of translation: a faithful one. It demands an attempt to be true to its truths, their traces. This is one level. One direction. One set among other sets. Grasp.

I embark, in the coming weeks, on a search for this poem in English, a search for every translation of this poem into English, and each seems to be at once entirely different and the same. I can see, for example, which lines or syntactic units were difficult to translate, which lines each translator struggled with. A few seem labored, wooden. Others seem perfunctory—safe. And a few, such as Daniel Simko's "version," are truly alive in the English—I can feel myself, reading, being written by this poem. Later, a German friend fluent in English looks over the translations, singles out this same translation by Simko, and says, "In terms of accuracy, this one here is one of the worst."

SUNKEN GARDENS

An offshore mound licks verbal oil.
Johnnie Cochran's phantoms have scattered.
Ferns guard the silver fuselage of an F16.

A future, tensed....
A brow-licking dachshund ... Democrats
Twitter within the fetus
Of a created
Ibix. Meanwhile, guys.
Moonbeams open throats into something more than
Food holes, Ford-tough

     such a wind

Only, as in sunken gardens

          the glass-black eyes
Of silver toads. Breathing militarized by sight.

÷

A DRAWN KNIFE

I am looking at his face. I am looking at his eyes. I am looking at someone I do not know, never could have known, since he died long before I was born. I look at his eyes, which seem small to me, too small, like the eyes of an animal, and then I wonder how or why eye-size ever came to represent levels of humanness, or compassion (the unusually large eyes of elephants and horses and whales are said "to have soul," whereas small eyes, "beady eyes," are often considered non-human or even non-mammalian—reptilian, cold). I'm trying to look at his eyes, and I am trying to write about looking at his eyes. I am doing two things, it seems, at once. Or three things. Since this is an image of a writer, I am seeing him—seeing in him—what I've read of and about him. I am seeing his image as a word, I am seeing words in his image (his words, the words of others). And then, fourthly, I am measuring what I know of these words against his face. In this sense I am reading him endlessly, and each time I am reading what I see, one of many, possible sights.

And what do I see? Above all, your gaze. It is fixed, for some reason, just above me, above the lens of the camera, perhaps at the one taking the photograph, at something beyond the camera, more likely at nothing. Your eyes, unlike the eyes of a subject looking directly at a camera, do not follow me around the room of my viewing. This trick occurs due to the flat surface of any pictorial representation, the surface of which never changes regardless of the angle to which you align your gaze. "Neigungswinkel," wrote Celan. Angle of inclination. By which we see the world. Your physician in the Krakow asylum reported that you often saw a man with a drawn knife standing behind your back. Even though your head faces forward, your gaze seems directed there, behind you. There is also something childlike about your posture, the slightly hunched shoulders, the weirdly knotted hands—as if tied that way, permanently—and above all the sense that your feet are not exactly touching the floor. Dangling. The posture of a child: *I will do this, but I am always somewhere else.*

ALL–SEEING SEALANT

Dear mannequin, pipeline, taurine gosling
Your strewn blossoms wilt
In the presence of gravity. Sun eidolons snag.
Think of a puppet without headedness.

O where in these scattered winter war zones
Are the angst-ridden voles, the....
An herbal-infused wind circles unborn dreams.
A dork mutters Milton. The green wagon

Is suffering around the bend
And to return from the region of likeness
One must learn to unravel April's wounds.

Mr. Leben, for example. He is not so tall,
Though his tubes protrude. (Aging, circles.)

Nuns wearing Diesel jeans embalm him in a ditch
While the Sameness Wand, still as a sternum, sails aloft.

We are two sternums, facing each other. Two ribcages. I do not know, at this hour, where the space my chest inhabits ends and his begins, where one language ends and another begins. Seen from the perspective of dreams (aerial, suspended, looking down at the room) I see the dots of our heads, divided by a narrow wooden table: a line, a border line, an equation. And then the things we say to each other, the things we write down, facing each other, and the words letter by letter held there and the notepad, and the thin yellow pencil moving back and forth over the border, because of the border, erasing it with our movements, our awareness of the border and our movements there.

One physician at the Krakow hospital reports that you have often seen, since childhood, a man with a drawn knife standing behind your back.

Yes. Everyone has their own relationship to the lyric tradition.

In your case, then, such a tradition would include the experience of fear?

No. Not fear.

What then?

Humility.

BLACKTRAKL

Autumn. Black striding by the forest's edge. Black metallic skies.
A shepherd leads a herd of black and red horses past her own
Black and empty sockets, her dirt-stiffened hair
Matted with black tears, O you shattered eyes in black mouths
Through black boughs the bells peal, two black horses
Prance in the meadows, a saint steps out of his black, painted wounds and
Carrying a rosy child a black angel in a black overcoat
Appears—O

Black angel, who quietly slipped from a tree's heart,
The black flight of birds always touches
The black dew, dripping from your temples, all roads flow into black decay . . .

Through her arms trickles black snow.
Decay flutters up on black wings. A black horse rears violently.
A fisherman pulls a huge, black fish from a starlit pond.
Someone whispering in the garden below; someone has deserted the black sky.

The dead
are the departed therefrom. Whose
leavings. Reading we partake of.

—Robert Duncan

IN AN ALTERNATE STOMACH

Ovaries dipped in gold. Steel-tipped semen.
Wallets crafted from the wings of swans.

In the heat a black hearse, shimmering.
Later, blue sand spills between the stars.

Her lichen-covered eyelids.
The small glass jars affixed to her lips.

Let the elegantly dressed boatman carry us across.
Let money like a swan on fire

Light the way out of this harmony.

I notice, for the first time since entering this room, the window just behind him. The surface of the glass reflects the room, his back, the light upon his back, which means it must be night here, or out there. Expecting to peer into a darkened landscape, trees, perhaps a back yard, a garden, or nothing, another wall, a brick wall, I rise and open the window. Instead, someone has darkened the window with black spray-paint. Instead: light like a visible wind rushes into my face. Instead: huge buildings, skyscrapers clothed in mirrored glass, some ending in skeletons of metal, steel, sections of pale, blue sky between them, clouds. We are in a city. We are high up and in a city—forty floors, fifty, all the floors reflecting other floors, other passageways, cubicles, rooms, other faces looking out of those rooms, reflected, turning away from their reflections. Knowing I am nowhere near the ground I feel suddenly dizzy. I shut the window. I sit down, but I am afraid to look up, look into his eyes, perhaps see the same urban scene, repeated in miniature, infinitely, or perhaps his eyes would simply mirror precisely what I saw, what sits across from him, speaks.

Sometimes, reading these poems, I'm reminded of what Artaud once said, that our minds are capable of an infinite number of tones, even ones that are inappropriate.

He didn't say that. He screamed it.

Can I ask you how the figure of the stranger functions in your poems? The stranger seems to be one who is always departing, always passing through, en route to somewhere else, traveling.

Never through, but around.

Why around?

It is not a gift. One has to walk out of one's self, one's city, into the outskirts, to meet him, her.

Your poems, and perhaps poetic language, record this journey?

Think instead of a large, yellow, breathing sponge.

You mean as "the image" of the stranger, the one standing before you, facing you?

I repeat. Think of a large, wet, breathing yellow sponge. Have you ever held one up to your ear?

No. But I was thinking about your poetics of decomposition, and how permeab—

Even a wet kitchen sponge. Squeeze it a little. The noise is deafening.

What persists despite efforts to translate around you, with you, read you, are the singular performances of decay and decomposition, as if intertextuality (meaning moving between texts) is materializing itself as an organic process, de- and re-composing itself, and each image, each instance, *a gentle orphan, her sweet body rotting in the bushes*—and if we are at any moment living and not-living, dead skin shed, fallen eyelashes, expired cells, thoughts, lost hair, letters, air, gas, how odd our systems of kinship, relatives, remembrance, blood relatives, race, systems that underwrite—*great word*—nation, nationality, fatherland, or mother tongue, *the same problem*, I know, let me finish this thought, *be my guest*, perhaps when I leave this room I should see myself as a corpse, a zombie, a limb thudding onto the floor, one soft eyeball rolling out, two, the word two, comma, syntax, too, *a word in time,* a way of coding, classifying, without which might we have a more visible way of seeing, up close, the cavernous size of our pores, the way the faces in Artaud's drawings are filled with soft, round, open holes, *like the mouths of orphans,* or any mouth, vent-mouth, *or any orifice,* that was unnecessary, *perhaps, but you're missing the point about decay,* how, *an orphan, dead, simply returns to the point of its arrival,* abandonment, *squared,* wounded kinship, *squared,* absence, *squared,* and to sing from such a position: unlike Orpheus, whose utterance-song is confined to the limits of specific loss, the utterance of a dead orphan is freed from a single binary, *it is a double loss,* and doubled it becomes the experience of doubles, where one can see, reflected on the surface of a pond—*allow me*—be my guest—*the angelic perversity of burning swans.*

ROSENCRANTZ: A WESTERN

Without a gesture or word of understanding
I am pulling, verbed and bent, a taut wire
Through the glazed, blue eyes of summer.

Then a glass leased from flung
Deigns to augment my life as a
She-male. Been there.

Done that. Lie down under another verb.
Counterfeit night puts its dawn-soaked lips
To my sternum. One can only eat, and keep eating.

No one home. Summer inheres.
A monad shells out sonatas
And Ewoks along some never-ending Walden.

The dense, inner weight of ferns is one way
You might light the interior of an ant's blue tunnel;
Otherwise, night's leaflessness trembles beside you,

Cruel as a starless branch. Therefore, the stranger
Trembles in the darkness. No Wind. Light's black furnace.
The silver voice in the mouth of a housefly.

REASONS WHY ORPHANS WEAR STILLNESS–MITTENS

1. It is difficult to think in the presence of an orphan.

2. It is difficult to think in the presence of the word "orphan."

3. It is like trying to think in the middle of an earthquake, trying to think about something other than what is happening, especially when what is happening is the repeated disturbance of the very ground of thought.

4. Some orphans become orphans, while others, despite being born, are born orphans, and still others are both born orphans and become orphans.

5. These orphaned orphans are the orphans with stillness-mittens (the ground is shaking).

6. When you meet an orphan and shake its hand, when one even obtains eye contact with such an orphan, one can feel, invisibly, the power of its stillness-mittens.

7. It is not a self-pitying power, which is a power owned by all other orphans.

8. It is not, in fact, anything like silence, anything like stillness, anything like coming upon an empty meadow the day after a heavy snow storm, a meadow that is no longer a meadow but simply an expanse, a white expanse, wind in the bordering birch trees, leafless, nothing around but your own breathing, your own pause, nothing around but the moment you realize this pause.

9. It is not even like any mitten, any category of mittenness.

10. How small a hyphen is. How effortless its great work.

÷

BERRIES IN THE DITCHES OF BRUEGEL

… a spotlight as moonlight, a lit face, the white splotches like clouds below the face, the face as cloud, drifting over the moon, or the sense that the forehead is not over-lit but just missing, erased. Within the genre of author portraits the profile is the most pretentious angle. Its perspective, gesture, and positioning (raised chin, as opposed to the shyness of a lowered chin) establish the illusion of the poet as visionary prophet, consumed, in the moment of image-capture, with some far-off, distant, other world. W. S. Hartshorn's famous frontal portrait of Poe derives its naked, crooked force not from the fact that the poet is unaware of how accurately his image will be recorded, but rather, since early silver-based photographic processes faded quickly, he seems unaware that it will ever last as a print, that it will circulate, be reproduced, end up splashed across a large cardboard display in Barnes & Noble—that it will, in short, ever be seen (just as he seems utterly broken, unable to see himself).

Here, you are entirely conscious, self-conscious—posing, or at least aware that the pose is what photographs simultaneously generate and capture. Barthes: "I project the present photograph's immobility upon the past shot, and it is this arrest which constitutes the pose … something *has passed* in front of the tiny hole and remained there forever." And I am strangely grateful that the beaded, feral intensity of your gaze—the sense, with almost every one of your portraits, that your eyelids, like the eyelids of dolls, are too open, unblinkingly open—is averted. Then I notice the ear. The ear with its lit lobe, its upper rim nearly pointed, elfish. I end up staring at this ear for a long time until my gaze travels through it, all the way to the ossicles, the three smallest bones in the human body, the incus, the malleus, then the stapes, which is shaped like a stirrup, or a small bird perch dangling in the middle of a cage. I see myself in miniature, sitting on this swing. I grab hold of the tiny bones. I push off, throw my legs out while leaning back. I try to swing within inches of your brain.

'Er the hands your white, gloved gestures
Trace in the night. We're bent above sunken Pfaden again.
When in thirst
Drink the icy, blue water
A sister, unseen, pulls from a turtle's lips.
Meanwhile, ruins whir under hazelbushes.
Insects search for lost body parts in the grass.
Stags through bars of moonlight refuse
To utter final statements, despite the pile of monocles
Spilling from a sprung briefcase. Yes,
Thank you for asking. Even the hands of she-males,
However nominal, itch.

NOCTURNE

Odors, unbequeathed. A tiered sheath
For the blue of error-stars, heaven's klieg light.
Gilded is the wagon instead.

Masks covered with night-lichen. A vent steams.
Unidentified a vent steams. History
A bubble forming on a sleeper's half-open lips.

O, one hour still of speech's warfare.
The sameness-wand, once more thrown aloft:
Fallen error-stars in the watery, tiered ears of angels.

Today I tell him what I saw during the morning, what I did. That I was among thousands upon thousands of people marching in the street—chanting, waving signs, singing, protesting. The gunmen with their guns, poised on the rooftops. The wooden, blue police barricades. The helicopters like tiny black video cameras hovering, then sliding sideways through the sky, following the avenue, the crowds. The food passed from hand to hand. The bottles of water. The chanting. The water-like movement of the crowd pouring down the avenue, always forward, small eddies of vocal protest forming, groups or nodes within the larger group, not an undifferentiated mob but a series of assemblages, points of view, political causes, bodies, vectors within the larger vector of the crowd. I know he is listening; his head is turned away, and his right ear, the ear I have gazed at in a photograph, faces me. But I suddenly feel unable to tell him that I also felt—marching, singing—a gnawing sense of despair. I knew, in my gut, that the largest world-wide anti-war protests in the history of civilization would have absolutely no effect, and I had nowhere to put this feeling. Which is why, afterwards, I immediately came here.

When you reported for active duty at the start of WWI you left for the train wearing a red carnation in your hat.

I had yet to see the black wolves break through the gates.

I don't really understand. You seemed to welcome if not war then the experience of warfare. In fact you asked to be sent to the front line several times.

Does one have a right to withdraw from hell? In any case, read your beloved Michaux: "Go to the ends of your errors, at least a few of them, to be able to study the type ... force that enemy—your structure—to show itself."

Yet today, marching, I felt somehow that it would accomplish nothing, that the war would go on despite us, all of us. It was an experience of pure powerlessness as a citizen, a citizen within a so-called democracy. I feel—felt—

Exposed. You were exposed. Didn't you announce, the moment you performed a perceptible act of resistance, your own powerlessness? You stepped into the gaze of the State and thereby gave it a choice: to pretend to incorporate your resistance, or ignore it.

Yes, but what other choice is there?

Discover a resistance you didn't know existed, that has no perceptible name.

Then what?

Disappear with it.

AMOUR WAR

Wanderer in a wind zoned by war; the moon-filter's red duration
Lights stillness. Wild voles
And fog cover the dirt hill;
Thin sternums, unwashed.

Of course: a word, a bombed-out hut, a hut-hole
Fluorescent gowns, emptied of fullness, rise from. Vertical
                                        birds
                                        suffer
                                        wind
                                        less
                                        ness and
A bent vernacular, a hand washing a photograph
As if water's softness alters
Anything in time.

INDENTED

Autumn sun, thin and unpredictable.
Herbert licks under under. The shadow
Of an orphan walks off into the afternoon.

Will blue raiment not burn
In either language? Starbucks,
For example. A half caff tall.

Such phrases spruce up
Our high-voltage pen.
In the next shot, red children,
And their vulgar songs pulling us
Into rooms of thunder.

Feeling the soft flight of madness
Orphans scatter, posing in the dusk as
Berries in the ditches of Bruegel.

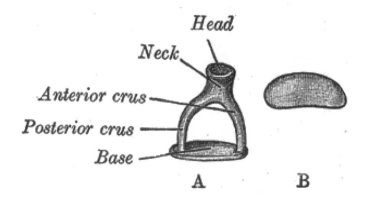

Head

Neck

Anterior crus

Posterior crus

Base

A   B

Face down on the table. A two-inch ceiling fan, which I'd never noticed, spins in the oblong puddle of drool that has leaked from my mouth. I hear my vision rewind mechanically to focus on its surface, floating specks of dust and colors and the wood's grain, magnified. I hear my eyes but it is the end of the dream that I am hearing, the weird clarity of our last conversation. At first I think that he is gone. His chair is empty. And then I realize that he is in the room, still in the room, behind me. It's the first time he has stood up and moved and this, I sense, is only because my eyes were closed, sleeping. I keep my head on the table. A speck-sized shadow moves across the pool of saliva. I hear him slide into the chair and light a cigarette. I lift my head.

Rilke wrote that to read you is "to experience vistas and insights as though pressed, an exile, against a pane of glass; for Trakl's life passes as in mirror images and fills its entire space, which cannot be entered, like the space of a mirror."

Repetition is the purest experience of form. My sister, for example....

Go on.

Let me tell you something: only when all adults—including brothers and sisters, fathers and daughters, mothers and sons, daughters and mothers, fathers and sons, sisters and sisters, brothers and brothers—are allowed to copulate, freely, without guilt, or fear of incarceration, or reproduction, will the world rid itself of nationalism.

You're referring to a post-human society, where kinship systems, since all children are essentially engineered, disappear? Cyborg orphans?

Heavenward steams the blood of the children murdered by Herod.

You're in a good mood today!

I loathe eye contact, physical contact with strangers, the sound of chewing, my own chewing, my own throat swallowing, and I also loathe those who—right when things were becoming interesting—are unable to stay awake. You think the dead are patient? You're wrong. We have no time. Your time is all anyone has in the world.

÷

A SIDE ROOM

A brow lowered in strict amazement
Often leads to sickness, to an imp
Stunned by its own hirsuteness (gender
Stores its delicacies in cool, rootless cellars).

And yet: his splendid knobs, scattered left/right.
Sic. And then X
Launches into a blue, bisexual sea
Of urgent sides and insides, night's gelatin, transparent,

Fur forming its own trembling game of hide and seek.
Reversal night, where blue ferns die of oxygen.
Even a submerged dock can be walked upon.
Even boats pull away from our hands like wild animals.

Voles hump under the Holland Tunnel; wonder follows
A white hand down blue holes. In the country of Pfad
Brown nuns sow wild oats
For the stillness-beasts
And here, on this side, red labs
Work out the glitches. Water leaks softly
From the blue eyes of a fly. Hirsute speech
Burns off into spores, chain stores.
Blueness augmented by this licking is not more sealed in blue.

A clock ticks in an abandoned, white cistern.

And the last unpolluted pond sinks further and further from filmic memory.

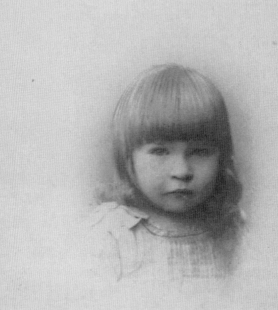

MAX BALDE   SALZBURG u WILDBAD GASTEIN.

1889. Two years old. The shutter opens. An image is recorded—a face, an object, a scene. And the moment the image exists it is freed of that instant, separated from it, and it passes through hands, in and out of albums, boxes, a frozen moment in time that moves through time and ends up in an archive in Innsbruck, slipped into a white manila folder which is, over a hundred years later, taken down, laid on a table, and slid across to me, the viewer, the viewer who, in another present already past, opened the folder and began to gaze.

It's your sister, I thought at first. And you answered: *It's me*. There was and is no detail that pricks, no wound (as Barthes would say) in this image. But the image, of you dressed as a girl stunned me. I became lost not in the image but in my own response to the image, a response which wanted to see this as visual proof that the figure of "the sister," which appears over and over— sixty times—in your poems, is more than a poetic effort to transfigure your beloved sister Greta into a Beatrice-like symbol of religious transcendence, is more than an intentionally shocking trope for incestuous desire, but is, in simple fact, another part of yourself, the Other of your self.

I resist this reading, however, when I approach the image through writing (this moment); I resist, essentially, myself, my subjective gaze. I want instead to situate the image historically, to let it be, simply, a record, a record that has nothing to do with me. I discover, through research, an odd sub-genre of late 19th century photography: children's portraiture. Boys "dressed" as girls. Since it was believed at the time that more boys died as infants than girls, they were—in order to trick fate—often dressed as girls before they were "breeched" (put into breeches) at the age of four or five. Experts in 19th century costumes and textiles argue, however, that this superstition no longer held sway in the 19th century; instead, boys were not dressed as girls, per se, but as children, and dresses, or "back-fastening gowns," were used for both genders for ease in diapering and toilet training. In contrast to the present, infancy was viewed in the late 19th century as an amorphous, genderless space—a pre-gendered space. And a boy's hair was often allowed to grow into long ringlets for two reasons. First, following Victorian conventions, an infant boy with long hair was thought to be a sign of wealth, of aristocracy (Little Lord Fauntleroy). Second, as a rite of passage from genderless infant to boy, a ringlet or "sausage curl" cutting-ceremony often took place, in which the mother cut off the curls, tied them together with a bow, and kept them as a memento.

You are, in this image, a child—simply that. It is the viewer, then, who looks back, who must translate the photograph against itself, translate time against itself, put the image back into time, back into a century, a country, a culture, back into the camera, the lens, the moment the shutter clicked and the location of the shutter when it clicked. There is nothing special about this photograph. Nothing special about children, either. Even photographs of children.

MENTION IT TO THE FURIOUS LUNGS

Under cracked sternums, verse-flung,
Ashcroft with his round, condom-colored eyes.
A brick of durable light rides
on the jagged back of a gelding.
Genet is a verisimilitude wolf, bending himself
into a form of verbal pantomime

and yet nothing

cries out from the mirrored chest
of St. Thomas

              lowering

his own hand
inside his own

Wonder//meat

If there is such a thing as a language of truth ... then this language of truth is—the true language. And this very language, whose divination and description is the only perfection a philosopher can hope for, is concealed in concentrated fashion in translations.

—Walter Benjamin
(translation: Harry Zohn)

One hand on the dog, the other on the fake railing. It is this other hand that eventually draws the eye. The arm, with its unlocatable elbow, seems oddly elongated, deformed. The sister, here, with you standing in the middle, is also a child, although the white skin still retains a hint of baby fat, a taut plumpness that contradicts her gaze, her decisively adult gaze.

The sister. In the context of a photograph, a document, something "that-has-been" (Barthes), it feels suddenly inappropriate to use such a noun, let alone a noun with a category-implying definite article, even though Trakl used this exact phrase over and over in his poems, and critics used it over and over in their prose. She is there. She is standing there. She stood there, has stood there, did stand there, stood. A photograph gathers every tense into its present. I look at the arm emerging from the puffed folds of the dress. The baby fingers. The bent wrist, holding weight—the only hint that she is actively lifting herself (has been asked to lift herself?) into the frame. Perhaps we can put her back—back into the photograph, back into her life, what little we know of it.

Even a name alone is a start.

Greta. Gretl. Margarethe.

Margarethe Trakl was the last of six children in the Trakl family, born when Georg was five, and they were close friends during childhood. Already the biographic tone slips in, the tone that brushes a life, the details of a life, under a phrase like "during childhood."

I could say, specifically, that their Alsatian governess taught Greta and Georg French, and it became their secret language (already they were translating; already children translate everything).

I could write a sentence like "Early on she displayed a gift for music."

I could quote other writers, other biographers, such as Francis Sharp, who uses, perfectly, the passive construction of biographic reportage: "She has been variously described at aggressive, hysterical, and pathologically eccentric."

I could say that it was this very eccentricity that Trakl loved, that he cherished—even looked up to, admired.

I could say that he always considered her the more talented sibling.

That they took drugs together, supplied by Georg, while they both were studying in Vienna, and that this was the beginning of her severe addiction problems.

I could provide dates about her life, I could provide facts.

I could present these to you in a form that conveys authority, certitude:

1891	Born on August 8th, the last of six children, to Tobias Trakl, a successful hardware dealer, and Maria.
1901	Attends boarding school at St. Pölten and in Vienna.
1908	Attends music academy in Vienna, where Georg is studying to become a pharmacist at the University of Vienna.
1910	Tobias Trakl dies, leaving family in financial ruin. Moves to Berlin to train with the composer and pianist Ernst von Dohnányi.
1912	July 17th. Marries bookseller Arthur Langen, 34 years her senior. Because of her age, Georg Trakl, now her legal guardian, authorizes the marriage.
1913	Possible affair with Erhard Buschbeck, a close friend of Trakl's.
1914	March. Trakl visits her in Berlin after she barely recovers from an abortion. Continued drug addiction. Unhappy marriage.
1914	November 3rd. Georg Trakl's death. A week before, in a letter to von Ficker, Trakl donates all of his belongings to her, including Wittgenstein's gift of 20,000 crowns.

1914-16   Husband leaves her. Unable to continue her career in music.

1917   September 23rd. Berlin. At a large party she steps into a side room and shoots herself.

A side room.

A private act in a public space.

A gesture—a grand gesture, tragic.

There is the question of music, her music.

A figure in a poem, a shadow.

Le jardin est vivant avec des bruits.

A public gesture in a public place.

The pianist sits down, adjusts the stool, finds the pedals, pauses.

She is there. She was standing there.

Even a name alone.

The garden is alive with noise.

A gesture, for example. Fingers raised above the keys.

And the space there. A room.

Already they were translating.

It is as if Barthes's idea of a punctum (a "sting, speck, cut," or "little hole" which rises out of the scene of the photograph, which "shoots out of it like an arrow, and pierces" the viewer) and his idea of an "excessive sign" have merged: the image swarms with little signs, seemingly burned marks, tears on the surface, swirling electrons, ash—all of which overflow it, spill out of it, noise. When I look at it I want to cover my ears (I can hear its madness; I can hear its set of contradictions: photographic permanence set against surface decay, set against Greta's youthfulness, set against her known mental instability, set against the Artaud-like burn-marks, set against her suicide, set against the nature of her suicide, set against...).

One thing, however, stabilizes. I don't know who took this image but I believe, judging from her gaze, that it was someone who loved her—or that she was, at the very least, thinking of that person when the shutter opened and light crowded the lens.

A HAND REACHED OUT TO ELIS

Elis, when the anvil of war lands, however softly, in Walden.
Elis, when the blackbird calls out in the dark forest,
Dissecting utterance into roving, uncommanded units ...
Remember,
That is your doom.
Your lips only trinkets—blue rims, mussel shells.

And when altitude bloats our legends,
When your forehead bleeds faintly
Into a stomach, starved of any stars, even crumbling stars,
When birds rise only by the rapid movement of their tongues—

Such white, written nights.
Yet with gentle footsteps you walk into the evening.
A vole purple with trauma breathes
In some far-off, shining, unregistered domain.

A thornbush rustles.
Monadic cinders
In the boy's moonlike eyes
Shed a white language of ash and absorption.
O Elis, how long ago did you die.

In a lab a hyacinth is used
To tint monocles and stem cells.
Softly bisexuals shift between trees.
At times a gentle animal emerges

As language, but only after
Language swings into view.

Something, perhaps the figure of a boy, or Greta, upsets him. I know enough to wait, to wait this out, the sudden lifelessness of his withdrawal, as if someone, somewhere, ripped a plug from the wall. Let the song remember the boy. His head is tilted down, and to the side. The current of one remaining electrode pulses, every two seconds, in the outer corner of his right eye. Each time it twitches I blink. The window for some reason is ajar; a wide, greedy slab of light carries noise, car horns, a helicopter, its low stutter, gone behind a building, returning, and below—not below—*you're still here*—within, within each noise another noise, a pigeon that swivels over the windshields of cabs, glass bottle thudding in an empty garbage can, snippets of cell phone conversations, "so what if your boss is watching you," even the presence of leaves, trees, a squirrel on a branch high over the sidewalks, pausing, one miniature hand always slightly raised, alert. I look at the books on the table, the editions, German editions, English. A name along the spine. An author.* A friend.

Is this a bad high school yearbook photo? I barely recognize you. I don't recognize you. Your face seems to be powdered, as if you were an actor dressing for a part, or an actor undressing after playing a part.

And that part in your hair is breathtaking. Majestic.

One could lose oneself in that part.

One could almost walk down it.

Travel it.

Be parted by it.

÷

NACHWORT

GRODEK

Am Abend tönen die herbstlichen Wälder
Von tödlichen Waffen, die goldnen Ebenen
Und blauen Seen, darüber die Sonne
Düstrer hinrollt; umfängt die Nacht
Sterbende Krieger, die wilde Klage
Ihrer zerbrochenen Münder.
Doch stille sammelt im Weidengrund
Rotes Gewölk, darin ein zürnender Gott wohnt
Das vergossne Blut sich, mondne Kühle;
Alle Straßen münden in schwarze Verwesung.
Unter goldnem Gezweig der Nacht und Sternen
Es schwankt der Schwester Schatten durch den schweigenden Hain,
Zu grüßen die Geister der Helden, die blutenden Häupter;
Und leise tönen im Rohr die dunkeln Flöten des Herbstes.
O stolzere Trauer! ihr ehernen Altäre
Die heiße Flamme des Geistes nährt heute ein gewaltiger Schmerz,
Die ungebornen Enkel.

GRODEK

In the evening the autumn woods resound
With deadly weapons, the golden plains
And blue lakes, over which more darkly
The sun rolls; night embraces
The dying warriors, the wild lament
Of their broken mouths.
Yet silently red clouds, inhabited by an angry god,
Gather below the willows
Spilled blood, lunar coolness.
All roads end in black decay.
Under the golden branches of night and stars
The sister's shadow sways through the silent grove
To greet the ghosts of heroes, the bleeding heads;
And the dark flutes of autumn play quietly in the reeds.
O prouder grief! you brazen altars
Today the hot flame of the spirit is fed by a violent pain,
The grandchildren—unborn.

Berlin, Germany
January 28, 2008

ACKNOWLEDGMENTS

Thanks to Creative Capital Foundation for its generous support of this project; thanks also to Eberhard Sauermann and Hans Weichselbaum for allowing access to and permission to reprint a few images from, respectively, the Brenner Archives in Innsbruck and the Georg-Trakl-Forschungs- und Gedenkstätte in Salzburg (note: save for a few rare portraits, most images and portraits were dragged off the internet); I'm grateful to Jesse Seldess at *Antennae* and everyone at The Corresponding Society for publishing earlier versions of these texts; special thanks to Anna Moschovakis, Genya Turovskaya, Matvei Yankelevich, James Copeland, Anastasia Skoybedo, and everyone at UDP for their conversation and *schöpferische Kraft*; most importantly, thanks to Uljana Wolf for her unwavering; finally, I want to acknowledge here Daniel Simko (1959-2004), whose incomparable versions of Trakl's poems haunt this book.

COLOPHON

This third printing of *Ventrakl* was printed and bound by McNaughton & Gunn in an edition of 700 copies with covers printed offset at Prestige Printing. The design is by Andreas Töpfer and goodutopian; typesetting by goodutopian using Bembo, Capibara and Hooge.

Ugly Duckling Presse is a 501(c)(3) not-for-profit publishing collective based in Brooklyn, NY, which specializes in poetry, translation, lost literature, aesthetics, performance, and books by artists.

This book is part of UDP's Dossier Series, which was created in 2008 to expand the formal scope of the Presse. Dossier books don't share a single genre or form but, rather, an investigative impulse. For more information about UDP and the Dossier Series, visit www.uglyducklingpresse.org.

CHRISTIAN HAWKEY has written two full-length collections of poetry (*The Book of Funnels* and *Citizen Of*), three chapbooks (*HourHour, Petitions for an Alien Relative, Ulf*), and a bilingual book of erasures, *Sonne from Ort*, made collaboratively with the German poet Uljana Wolf, with whom he also translates Ilse Aichinger. In 2006 he received a Creative Capital Innovative Literature Award. In 2008 he was a DAAD Artist-in-Berlin Fellow. His work has been translated into more than a dozen languages, including English.